First World War
and Army of Occupation
War Diary
France, Belgium and Germany

58 DIVISION
175 Infantry Brigade
London Regiment
2/9 Battalion
1 September 1915 - 23 February 1916

WO95/3009/2

The Naval & Military Press Ltd
www.nmarchive.com
Published in association with The National Archives

Published by

The Naval & Military Press Ltd

Unit 10 Ridgewood Industrial Park,

Uckfield, East Sussex,

TN22 5QE England

Tel: +44 (0) 1825 749494

www.naval-military-press.com

www.nmarchive.com

This diary has been reprinted in facsimile from the original. Any imperfections are inevitably reproduced and the quality may fall short of modern type and cartographic standards.

© Crown Copyright
Images reproduced by permission of The National Archives, London, England, 2015.

Contents

Document type	Place/Title	Date From	Date To
Heading	WO95/3009/2/3		
Heading	58 Division 175 Bde 2/9 London Regt 1915 Sept-1916 Feb (Uk) 1917 Feb-1918 Jan Absorbed By 1/9 Bn Feb 18		
Heading	WO95/3009/2 1915 Sep-1916 Feb 2/9 London Reg		
Miscellaneous	War Diary Statement		
War Diary	Melton	01/09/1915	30/09/1915
Heading	War Diary Of 2/9th Bn London Regiment From 1st October 1915 To 31st October 1915		
War Diary	Bromeswell Camp Melton	01/10/1915	27/10/1915
War Diary	Ipswich	28/10/1915	30/11/1915
Heading	War Diary Of 2/9th Bn London Regt From 1-12-15 To 31-12-15		
War Diary	Ipswich	01/12/1915	23/02/1916

WO95
3009/2
/3

58 DIVISION

175 BDE

2/9 LONDON REGT

1915 SEPT — 1916 FEB (UK)

1917 FEB — 1918 JAN

(ABSORBED BY 1/9 BN FEB 18)

WO 95
3009/2

1915 Sep - 1916 Feb

2/9 London Reg

War Diary Statement

1/9/15

Unit. 2/9th. Battn. London Regt.
Brigade. 175th. Inf. Bde
Division 58th (London) Div
Mob. Centre London

Temp. War Station   Melton - Woodbridge

Stations occupied
subsequent to   Crowborough -
Concentration   Ipswich -
                   Melton

———

Report Nil

P. E. L. Parry
Major
for Lt. Col
Commanding

Army Form C. 2118.

WAR DIARY
INTELLIGENCE SUMMARY.
(Erase heading not required.)

Instructions regarding War Diaries and Intelligence Summaries are contained in F.S. Regs., Part II. and the Staff Manual respectively. Title pages will be prepared in manuscript.

Hour, Date, Place	Summary of Events and Information	Remarks and references to Appendices
Mullets		
1st September 1915	2nd RWN	
2nd	2nd RWN	
3rd	2nd RWN	
4th	2nd RWN	
5th	2nd RWN	
6th	Hostile aircraft reported on right 6th – 9th. Neither seen on heard	
7th	Hostile aircraft reported 7th – 8th. Neither seen on heard. RWN	
8th	Battalion took up allotted position RWN	
9th	Higher of 8th & 9th as assigned of 7th & 8th RWN	
9th	2nd RWN	
10th	2nd RWN	

WAR DIARY
or
INTELLIGENCE SUMMARY.
(Erase heading not required.)

Army Form C. 2118.

2

Hour, Date, Place	Summary of Events and Information	Remarks and references to Appendices
Mellis		
11th September 1915	night 11th–12th Hostile aircraft reported/visible seen on allotted position, kept up allotted position. RfW	
12th "	Hostile aircraft heard going E. hutts of the Camp on night 12th–13th RfW	
13th "	Major Davis, president of Court Martial held at Hypo 2/10th Bn. London Regt to try Pte 2380 Pte W. Hutton 2/10th Bn. Capt R.N. Johnson attended as for instruction. night of 13th–14th Battalion kept up allotted position for aircraft. Aircraft and Zeppelins(?) from Lewes better heard and seen. RfW	
14th "	Nil RfW	
15th "	Capt R.N. Johnson member of District Court-Martial held at Hypo 2/11th Bn. London Regt to try 2u 3434 Pte F.C. Rafell 2/11th Bn. Lt M. Loran attended for instruction. Battalion kept up allotted position or report of aircraft on nights 15th–16th. Aircraft neither seen or heard RfW	

Army Form C. 2118.

3

WAR DIARY
INTELLIGENCE SUMMARY.
(Erase heading not required.)

Instructions regarding War Diaries and Intelligence Summaries are contained in F. S. Regs., Part II. and the Staff Manual respectively. Title pages will be prepared in manuscript.

Hour, Date, Place	Summary of Events and Information	Remarks and references to Appendices
Mellón		
16th September 1915	nil RQW	
17th "	Period of vigilance commenced 6.15 pm RQW	
18th "	Period of vigilance terminated 3.20 pm RQW	
19th "	nil RQW	
20th "	nil RQW	
21st "	nil RQW	
22nd "	Receipt of Central force A D 940 calling of way in which numbers other ranks available for draft RQW	
23rd "	Reply to above 217 all specialists RQW	
24th "	nil RQW	
25th "	nil RQW	
26th "	nil RQW	

Army Form C. 2118.

WAR DIARY
or
INTELLIGENCE SUMMARY.
(Erase heading not required.)

Hour, Date, Place	Summary of Events and Information	Remarks and references to Appendices
Mellor		
27th September 1915	Nil Return	
28th "	" "	
29th "	" "	
30th "	" "	

A.W. Berry Lt Colonel Commanding 2/1 1th Bn London Reg.

Army Form C. 2118.

WAR DIARY
or
INTELLIGENCE SUMMARY.
(Erase heading not required.)

Instructions regarding War Diaries and Intelligence Summaries are contained in F.S. Regs., Part II and the Staff Manual respectively. Title pages will be prepared in manuscript.

Hour, Date, Place	Summary of Events and Information	Remarks and references to Appendices
	Confidential War Diary of 2/9th Bn London Regiment from 1st October 1915 to 31st October 1915-	

[Stamp: 58th (2/2nd LONDON) DIVISION — GENERAL STAFF — 3 NOV 1915]

Army Form C. 2118.

WAR DIARY
INTELLIGENCE SUMMARY
(Erase heading not required.)

Instructions regarding War Diaries and Intelligence Summaries are contained in F.S. Regs., Part II. and the Staff Manual respectively. Title pages will be prepared in manuscript.

[Stamp: LONDON DIVISION / 3 - NOV 1915 / GENERAL STAFF]

Hour, Date, Place	Summary of Events and Information	Remarks and references to Appendices
Bromewell Camp Mellor		
1 - 10 - 15	nil R.S.W.	
2 - 10 - 15	nil R.S.W.	
3 - 10 - 15	nil R.S.W.	
4 - 10 - 15	District Court Martial on No 3585 Pte J. Butler, 2/10th Bn London Regt. Capt. K. W. Johnson a member. Lt M. Loram attended for instruction. Aircraft reported on night 4-5. Battalion took up position - neither seen or heard. R.S.W.	
5 - 10 - 15	Lt M. Loram attended D.C.M. for instruction at H.Qrs 2/10th Bn London Regt - R.S.W.	
6 - 10 - 15	nil R.S.W.	
7 - 10 - 15	D.C.M. on No 2316 Cpl H. Platt 2/11th Bn London Regt. Capt. G. Jolley a member - Lt. M. Loram attended for instruction. R.S.W.	

Army Form C. 2118.

2

WAR DIARY
INTELLIGENCE SUMMARY.
(Erase heading not required.)

Instructions regarding War Diaries and Intelligence Summaries are contained in F.S. Regs., Part II. and the Staff Manual respectively. Title pages will be prepared in manuscript.

Hour, Date, Place	Summary of Events and Information	Remarks and references to Appendices
8 - 10 - 15	nil R.S.N.	
9 - 10 - 15	nil R.S.N.	
10 - 10 - 15	nil R.S.N.	
11 - 10 - 15	nil R.S.N.	
12 - 10 - 15	nil R.S.N.	
13 - 10 - 15	night 13-14 - aircraft warning - battalion both up position. 2 airships seen at 11.25 p.m and 1.20 a.m respectively travelling N.E. R.S.N.	
14 - 10 - 15	nil R.S.N.	
15 - 10 - 15	nil R.S.N.	
16 - 10 - 15	nil R.S.N.	
17 - 10 - 15	nil R.S.N.	
18 - 10 - 15	D.C.M. on 20.1640 Pte J.C. Edwards 2/10th Bn Lincoln Regt. Major P.L. d'A Parry Regt. Capt. G.B. Schilt a member - Mr W.A. Carter President for instruction R.S.N.	

Army Form C. 2118.

3

WAR DIARY
INTELLIGENCE SUMMARY.
(Erase heading not required.)

Instructions regarding War Diaries and Intelligence Summaries are contained in F. S. Regs., Part II. and the Staff Manual respectively. Title pages will be prepared in manuscript.

Hour, Date, Place	Summary of Events and Information	Remarks and references to Appendices
19-10-15	Nil. R.W.	
20-10-15	Aircraft warning 10.20 am. Battalion took up position. R.W.	
21-10-15	Nil R.W.	
22-10-15	Nil R.W.	
23-10-15	Capt. G. Jolley member of board of officers at Supply Depot, WOODBRIDGE. Capt. W. P. Krillin member of Court of enquiry at MELTON HUTMENTS. R.W.	
24-10-15	Nil R.W.	
25-10-15	Nil R.W.	
26-10-15	Nil R.W.	
27-10-15	On night 27-28 Battalion took up aircraft position on receipt of warning - nothing seen or heard. R.W.	

Army Form C. 2118.

WAR DIARY
INTELLIGENCE SUMMARY.
(Erase heading not required.)

4

Hour, Date, Place	Summary of Events and Information	Remarks and references to Appendices
Ipswich 28-10-15	Battalion moved into billets at IPSWICH by march route R.N.	
29-10-15	nil R.N.	
30-10-15	nil R.N.	
31-10-15	nil R.N.	

A.R.Nunn
Lt. Colonel
Commdg 2/9th Bn. London Regt.

2/4th Bn.

Army Form C. 2118.

WAR DIARY
or
INTELLIGENCE SUMMARY.
(Erase heading not required.)

Instructions regarding War Diaries and Intelligence Summaries are contained in F.S. Regs., Part II and the Staff Manual respectively. Title pages will be prepared in manuscript.

CENTRAL REGISTRY -6 DEC 1915

Hour, Date, Place	Summary of Events and Information	Remarks and references to Appendices
IPSWICH		
1-11-15	nil r&m.	
2-11-15	nil r&m.	
3-11-15	District Court martial at the Barracks on No 79129 Bomba. G. HALL - 4th(R) Batt. R.F.A. Capt. K.W. JOHNSON a member Lt. W.N. CARTER attendn for instruction r&m.	
4-11-15	nil r&m.	
5-11-15	nil r&m.	
6-11-15	nil r&m.	
7-11-15	nil r&m.	
8-11-15	nil r&m.	
9-11-15	nil r&m.	
10-11-15	nil r&m.	
11-11-15	nil r&m.	

WAR DIARY
—or—
INTELLIGENCE SUMMARY.
(Erase heading not required.)

Army Form C. 2118.

2

CENTRAL REGISTRY - 6 DEC 1915

Hour, Date, Place	Summary of Events and Information	Remarks and references to Appendices
IPSWICH		
12 - 11 - 15	Nil R/W.	
13 - 11 - 15	Court of Enquiry at Headquarters (Battn) to enquire into illegal absence of No. 5167. Rfn F. LOVEGROVE. President Capt G. TOLLEY. Members Lieut L.M.CALVERT and 2nd Lieut H.S.PRINCE. R/W.	
14 - 11 - 15	Nil R/W.	
15 - 11 - 15	District Court-Martial at Headquarters 2/10 th Bn LONDON Regt on No. 124 Sergt J. BARDELL. 2/10 th Bn LONDON Regt. Capt G. TOLLEY a member. Capt G.F.GRIFFITH attended for instruction. District Court-martial at The Barracks on No 12769 Sgt. W.G. WHEATLEY. 5th (R) Batt. R.F.A. Lieut M. LOA Malta did for instruction The undermentioned NCOs and men discharged for re-enlistment into the R.F.C. 2212. L/Cpl. KNIGHT 1882 Rfn FULLER 3191. Rfn. STEVENS 1733 L/Cpl ALFORD	

Army Form C. 2118.

WAR DIARY
INTELLIGENCE SUMMARY.
(Erase heading not required.)

Hour, Date, Place	Summary of Events and Information	Remarks and references to Appendices
IPSWICH 15-11-15 (cont)	5060 Rfn Ryan 2893 L/Cpl. DUNKLEY 3204 " ADAMS 3316 Rfn. TAYLOR 3775 " TAYLOR 3776 " PORTER 4039 " ROGERS 2430 L/Cpl CULVERHOUSE 3557 " HUMPHREY 2754 Rfn. FAIRCHILD 3474 " FYSH 3164 " COATSWORTH 4700 " MORTIMER 2109 " BENNETT R.S.N.	
16-11-15	2nd R.S.N.	
17-11-15	2nd R.S.N.	
18-11-15	2nd R.S.N.	
19-11-15	2nd R.S.N.	
20-11-15	2nd R.S.N.	
21-11-15	2nd R.S.N.	
22-11-15	Field Genl Court martial at Ile Bernache on 203878 Gunner M. GILL R.F.A. Capt W.P. WILTON a member. Capt G.F. GRIFFITH attached for instruction. R.S.N.	

WAR DIARY
INTELLIGENCE SUMMARY

Army Form C. 2118
4

Hour, Date, Place	Summary of Events and Information	Remarks and references to Appendices
IPSWICH 23-11-15	District Court-martial at Headquarters 2/10th Bn LONDON Regt on No 3566. Pte. J. CONUP. 2/10th Bn. LONDON Regt. President Major P.E.L. PARRY. Capt. G. TULLEY a member. Lieut M. LOAM attached for instruction R&W	
24-11-15	nil rept	
25-11-15	Court of Enquiry at Headquarters 2/3rd LONDON Bde. R.F.A. Major R. Ft. DAVIES. President. ditto R&W	
25-11-15	nil rept	
26-11-15	nil R&W	
27-11-15	District Court-martial at Ile Barracks on No 51354 Driver G. MORSE. R.F.A. Lieut C.M. SANKEY attached for instruction R&W	
28-11-15	nil R&W	
29-11-15	nil R&W	
30-11-15	District Court-martial at Ile Barracks on No 32907 Gunner J. PRICE 1st B Reserve Brigade R.F.A	

Army Form C. 2118.

WAR DIARY
or
INTELLIGENCE SUMMARY.
(Erase heading not required.)

Instructions regarding War Diaries and Intelligence Summaries are contained in F.S. Regs., Part II. and the Staff Manual respectively. Title pages will be prepared in manuscript.

5

Hour, Date, Place	Summary of Events and Information	Remarks and references to Appendices
IPSWICH 30-11-15 (cont)	Capt. K.W. JOHNSON a member Lieut W.N. CARTER attended for instruction	[signature] Lt Col. Arnold 2/9th Bn London Regt

Army Form C. 2118.

WAR DIARY
INTELLIGENCE SUMMARY.
(Erase heading not required.)

Hour, Date, Place	Summary of Events and Information	Remarks and references to Appendices
	Confidential War Diary of 2/9th Bn London Regt from 1-12-15 to 31-12-15	

Instructions regarding War Diaries and Intelligence Summaries are contained in F.S. Regs., Part II. and the Staff Manual respectively. Title pages will be prepared in manuscript.

(73989) W4141—463. 400,000. 9/14. H.&J.Ltd. Forms/C. 2118/10.

Army Form C. 2118.

WAR DIARY
or
INTELLIGENCE SUMMARY.
(Erase heading not required.)

Instructions regarding War Diaries and Intelligence Summaries are contained in F. S. Regs., Part II and the Staff Manual respectively. Title pages will be prepared in manuscript.

Hour, Date, Place	Summary of Events and Information	Remarks and references to Appendices
IPSWICH		
1 - 12 - 15	nil return	
2 - 12 - 15	nil return	
3 - 12 - 15	nil return	
4 - 12 - 15	nil return	
5 - 12 - 15	nil return	
6 - 12 - 15	nil return	
7 - 12 - 15	nil return	
8 - 12 - 15	nil return	
9 - 12 - 15	District Court-Martial at the Barracks on 2nd 110615 Driver A.G. CLARKE 1st "B" Reserve F.A. Brigade charge:- M. SANKEY attending for instruction Court of enquiry at Holyp 12/10th Bn London Regt- in damage to gateway. President-Major R.F. DAVIES Capt. G. TOLLE # a member RAM	
10. 12. 15	District Court-Martial at WARREN HEATH CAMP on No 16411 Gunner G. P. WORTON 2/1st F.A. Brigade	

WAR DIARY

INTELLIGENCE SUMMARY.

(Erase heading not required.)

Army Form C. 2118.

2

Hour, Date, Place	Summary of Events and Information	Remarks and references to Appendices
IPSWICH		
10-12-15 (cont)	Capt. W.P. WILTON & another. 2nd Lt H.D. BLACKBURNE attending for instruction. R.M.	
11-12-15	nil R.M.	
12-12-15	nil R.M.	
13-12-15	nil R.M.	
14-12-15	nil R.M.	
15-12-15	District Court-martial at WARREN HEATH CAMP on No 1992 Driver A.M. TAYLOR 2/1st F.A. Brigade 2nd Lieut. T.C. BRANDRAM attending for instruction.	
16-12-15	District Court-martial at Headquarters 2/11th Bn LONDON Regt. on No 1866 Bugler L BOWLES. 2/11th Bn LONDON Regt Capt. W.P. WILTON & another. 2nd Lieut E. SHAND attending for instruction. Regimental Court of Enquiry on to damage to a motor car. President Major P.E.L. PARRY members { 2nd Lt. T.C. BRANDRAM { G.C. ALLEN R.M.	

WAR DIARY
or
INTELLIGENCE SUMMARY.
(Erase heading not required.)

Army Form C. 2118.

3

Instructions regarding War Diaries and Intelligence Summaries are contained in F.S. Regs., Part II. and the Staff Manual respectively. Title pages will be prepared in manuscript.

Hour, Date, Place	Summary of Events and Information	Remarks and references to Appendices
IPSWICH		
17-12-15	2nd RWF	
18-12-15	2nd RWF	
19-12-15	2nd RWF.	
20-12-15	Court of Enquiry at Batta. Headquarters to enquire into damage done to a stove and lantern by transport wagon. President, Major P.E.L. PARRY. Members 2nd Lt T.C. BRANDRAM 2nd Lt G.C. ALLEN R.W.	
21-12-15	Court of Enquiry at Batta Headquarters to enquire into damage done the illegal absence of No. 5405 Rfn. W.R.J. FOSTER. President Major R. H. DAVIES. Members Lieut- C.M. SANKEY RW 2nd Lt. L.W. BULL	

Army Form C. 2118.

WAR DIARY
or
INTELLIGENCE SUMMARY.
(Erase heading not required.)

Instructions regarding War Diaries and Intelligence Summaries are contained in F. S. Regs., Part II and the Staff Manual respectively. Title pages will be prepared in manuscript.

4

Hour, Date, Place	Summary of Events and Information	Remarks and references to Appendices
IPSWICH		
22-12-15	nil rqm	
23-12-15	nil rqm	
24-12-15	nil rqm	
25-12-15	nil rqm	
26-12-15	nil rqm	
27-12-15	nil rqm	
28-12-15	nil rqm	
29-12-15	nil rqm	
30-12-15	nil rqm	
31-12-15	nil rqm	

P.E.L. Carr
Major for Lt Col Commdg
2/9th 13th Bn London Regt

2/9th Bn. LONDON Regt.

WAR DIARY
INTELLIGENCE SUMMARY.
(Erase heading not required.)

Army Form C. 2118.

Instructions regarding War Diaries and Intelligence Summaries are contained in F.S. Regs., Part II and the Staff Manual respectively. Title pages will be prepared in manuscript.

[Stamp: 58th LONDON DIVISION – 3 FEB. 1916 – GENERAL STAFF]

Hour, Date, Place	Summary of Events and Information	Remarks and references to Appendices
IPSWICH		
22-1-16	Capt. S.V. SHEA transferred to 3/9th Bn London Regt. R.W.	
28-1-16	Battalion took up allotted position against hostile aircraft at about 10.0 p.m. returning to quarters at 12 midnight. No aircraft seen or heard R.W.	

R.G. Warren
Capt & Adjt
2/9th Bn LONDON Regt

2/9th Bn LONDON Regt. Q.V.R.

WAR DIARY

INTELLIGENCE SUMMARY.
(Erase heading not required.)

Army Form C. 2118.

Instructions regarding War Diaries and Intelligence Summaries are contained in F.S. Regs., Part II. and the Staff Manual respectively. Title pages will be prepared in manuscript.

Hour, Date, Place	Summary of Events and Information	Remarks and references to Appendices
IPSWICH		
2-2-16	Under instructions from 5-8th DIVN. small posts sent out to arrest certain motor car. posts shortly afterwards recalled. No arrest made. R.G.W.	
4-2-16	draft of 104 other ranks received from 3/9th Bn LONDON Regt R.G.W.	
10-2-16	23 other ranks transferred to 1/1st LONDON Divisional Cyclist Company R.G.W.	
23-2-16	2nd Lieut H. DAVIES. 9th Bn OXFORD & BUCKS. L.I. left to re-join his unit. R.G.W.	

R. G. Kanen
Capt & Adjt
2/9th Bn LONDON Regt.
Q.V.R.

www.ingramcontent.com/pod-product-compliance
Lightning Source LLC
Chambersburg PA
CBHW081505160426
43193CB00014B/2599